Safety

Jean Harrison

Published by Evans Brothers Limited in association with Save the Children UK.

Evans Brothers Limited.
2A Portman Mansions
Chiltern Street
London W1U 6NR

First published 2004

British Library Cataloguing in Publication Data
Harrison, Jean
    Safety. - (Children's Rights)
    1. Accidents - Prevention - Juvenile literature
    2. Childrens abuse - Prevention - Juvenile literature
    3. Children's rights - Juvenile literature
    I. Title
    323.3'52

ISBN 0 237 525526

Printed in China

Credits:
Series editor: Louise John
Editor: Nicola Edwards
Designer: Simon Borrough
Producton: Jenny Mulvanny

Acknowledgements
Cover: Kalpesh Lathigra
Title page: Kalpesh Lathigra
p6: Brendan Paddy/Save The Children UK
p7: Stuart Freedman/Network
p8: Dan White/Save The Children UK
p9: Anne Heslop
p10: Michael Amendolia/Network
p11a: Michael Amendolia/Network
p11b: Michael Amendolia/Network
p12: Michael Amendolia/Network
p13: Michael Amendolia/Network
p14: Tim Hetherington/Network
p15a: Tim Hetherington/Network
p15b: Tim Hetherington/Network
p16: Sebastian Rich/Save The Children UK
p17: Jenny Matthews
p18: Tim Hetherington/Network
p19: Tim Hetherington/Network
p20: Stephen Lewis
p21: Dario Mitidieri
p22: Kalpesh Lathigra
p23: Kalpesh Lathigra
p24: Howard Davies
p25a: Michael Amendolia/Network
p25b: Dan White
p26: Stuart Freedman/Network
p27a: Stuart Freedman/Network
p27b: Stuart Freedman/Network

Contents

All children have rights

The history of rights for children In 1919, a remarkable woman called Eglantyne Jebb founded the Save the Children Fund. She wanted to help children who were dying of hunger as a result of the First World War. Four years later, she wrote a very special set of statements, a list of children's rights. Eglantyne Jebb said that her aim was "to claim certain rights for children and labour for their universal recognition". This meant that she wanted worldwide agreement on children's rights.

It was many years before countries around the world agreed that children have rights, but eventually the statements became recognised in international law in 1989. They are known as the United Nations Convention on the Rights of the Child (UNCRC). The rights in the UNCRC are based on the idea that everyone deserves fair treatment.

The UNCRC is a very important document. Almost every country in the world has signed it, so it relates to most of the world's children. The rights listed in the UNCRC cover all areas of children's lives such as their right to have a home and their right to be educated.

In times of war, families, like this one in Afghanistan, can find it hard to protect their children from the dangers that are around them.

Rights for all? The UNCRC should mean that the rights of children everywhere are guaranteed. However, this is not the case. Every day, millions of children are denied their rights. Children suffer discrimination because they are poor, or disabled, or because they work for a living. It might be because of their religion, race or whether they are a boy or a girl.

Children are very vulnerable, so they need special care and protection. The UNCRC exists to try to make sure that they are protected.

The right to feel safe Many of the Articles in the UNCRC are about every child's right to feel safe and protected. When children feel safe, they are able to grow into healthy and useful citizens. Here are some of the Articles:

Article 19 You have the right to protection from injury, violence, abuse and neglect.

Article 22 You have the right to special protection and help if you are a refugee.

Article 32 You have the right to protection from work that is bad for your health or education.

Article 38 You have the right not to be in an army or fighting in a war before you are 15. If you are affected by war you must be protected.

Save the Children Save the Children UK is part of the International Save the Children Alliance working in over 100 countries worldwide to make children's rights a reality. This book and the others in the series tell the stories of children around the world who are achieving their rights with the help of Save the Children projects.

7

Children who are poor have the right to be safe

"There's a lot of fighting around here – so much you sometimes can't even go out of your house." Juan, 9, Colombia

Feeling safe It is important for everybody to live in safety, not just those who have money. It is particularly important for children to live in places where they are protected from danger. Children need people who will look after them if they hurt themselves or if they are afraid or in danger. It is the children from poor families who are most often denied their right to live safely.

Unsafe places Children who are poor are more likely to live in unsafe places. The building they live in may be poorly constructed, or old and falling down. It may be in an area where there are dangerous chemicals or on land that is likely to flood and so is unsuitable for houses. In places like this, the rent is lower so people who have little money are more likely to go there to live. Children who live in dangerous places are more likely to become ill or have accidents.

Leaving home Some children leave home because they are badly treated or because their parents can't afford to look after them. In many big cities across the world, children live on the streets, where their health and safety are at risk.

This family in East Timor, where a peace-keeping force is needed, struggle to give their children a safe place to live.

Many children's lives are affected when there is an emergency in their country. In times of war, or when there is a disaster such as an earthquake or a flood, it can become too dangerous to stay at home so they have to find a safer place to live until the emergency is over.

Dangerous jobs   Many poor children have to work – sometimes in dangerous conditions. Their employer may not provide machinery and tools that are safe to use, or give them special clothing and equipment, such as goggles, that protect them from harmful chemicals, sounds or lights. Children particularly are likely to become ill when they live or work in poor conditions, because their bodies are still growing and need extra care.

Feeling scared   Children can easily become frightened, especially if other people treat them badly. All children have the right to be looked after and protected by adults.

Bad weather and disasters can rob children of a safe place to live. This family has found a temporary home after an earthquake destroyed their home in Gujerat, India.

Cristian's story

Eleven-year-old Cristian lives in Medellin, a city in the South American country of Colombia. It is one of the most violent places in the world. Cristian's home is in a part of town where gangs fight each other, mainly over drugs and money.

One day Cristian was out with his mum when they saw some young men with guns run down the road. Cristian realised they were gang members and he hurried his mum inside the house. A few minutes later they heard shooting and not long after that the police came. The gang members had shot a man and he had died. Cristian was very frightened, but relieved that he and his mum had got out of the way.

Many people in the neighbourhood were getting really worried about the gangs. They saw that the children were copying the gang members, fighting and bullying each other.

Cristian practises basketball shots with his friends Wilmer and Juan in the safety of the school playground.

So the schoolteachers started a project, supported by Save the Children, called *Living Together*. Through this project the children began to learn to respect each other, even when they disagreed about things. They learned to talk to each other and to work together to solve their problems.

Cristian was chosen to be a class representative and attend some workshops. When he came back to his class he told the other children what he had learned. Then they all tried to put the ideas into action.

One day Cristian was very brave. He saw two boys pretending to strangle each other. Some other boys were trying to get them to fight each other properly. So Cristian did a very strange thing. He threw a bucket of cold water over them. The shock of the water was so great that the boys stopped fighting for a minute. Then Cristian said, "Don't fight any more – if you stop now, you'll soon forget about it and become friends again."

And that is exactly what happened. Cristian and his friends are much happier now they are learning how to make life safer for themselves and their families.

The children have learned to play together without fighting each other.

Cristian says, "I think my community can get rid of the gangs if people change and children are told to talk instead of fighting."

Children who work have the right to be safe

Twelve-year-old Anh sells lottery tickets in the market district of Ho Chi Minh City in Vietnam.

The need to work Most children work because they need to – their families need the money they earn to survive. Not all child labour is harmful. Some children stay at home and help with the family business, which might be a farm or a shop. Only about one out of twenty working children produces goods for export. Most work in family homes or businesses or as street traders.

Health and safety In the more developed countries such as the UK there are very strict 'health and safety' laws to protect everyone in their places of work, in shops and in other public places. Some countries do not have such laws, or are too poor to enforce them. Some employers are more interested in making money than in making sure the workers are protected. So many people, including children, in less developed countries such as India or Mali, have to work in unsafe conditions.

"I don't like the work at all, but we wouldn't be able to eat if I didn't work." Guddi, 16, India

12

Unsafe working conditions Some children are exploited because they have to work full-time when they are very young, or are not paid fairly for their work or are not treated as human beings.

They may have to work long hours with no proper breaks and in places where there is little fresh air. The long hours mean that the children cannot go to school or are too tired to learn. They may have little time to relax and play. Some of the materials the children work with may be dangerous and make them ill. Children like Guddi from India work in small, dark, airless rooms heating glass bangles over a hot flame.

Away from home

Children, such as those who make carpets in India and Pakistan, sometimes have to leave home to work. Some of them have even been kidnapped or sold, and taken far away from home to provide cheap labour for their employers.

Finding a better life

Projects have been set up to improve the lives of working children. They help families to find ways of earning more money, and help the children go to school so that they can get proper jobs when they are grown up.

Fabiana and her friend Ilka in Brazil both work as child-minders although they are still children themselves.

Amadou's story

Amadou approached the hillside cautiously. He was the first to arrive at the goldmine in Burkina Faso, West Africa where he spent several hours every day underground. Would there be any problems today? The entrance to the mine was just a narrow hole in the ground. So many children went through it each day that the edges had had to be strengthened with sandbags. But if the sandbags became loose and fell into the mine, there would be no way out for anyone inside.

Amadou adjusted the torch tied to his head and carefully lowered himself through the rough opening. He paused for a moment to let his eyes adjust to the darkness inside. He felt his way carefully down the shaft. He was looking for rocks that might have grains of gold in them. He had to hack the rocks from the sides of the shaft and carry them up to the surface, then take them home to be crushed. Constant digging into the sides of the shaft to get the rocks out had made huge holes and even tunnels. Once or twice the top had caved in and rocks and soil tumbled down. When that happened, Amadou could only

The entrance to the mine is narrow and dangerous.

wait for the dust to settle and then dig up towards the surface, hoping that the way out had not been blocked.

Amadou had not been going down the mines for long. He used to watch his parents digging there and then go down secretly after the adults had all left. Now he was ten years old and his parents had agreed that he was old enough to do this dangerous work. So the adults now looked after the cattle and the boys went down the mine. Amadou's elder sisters helped to crush the rocks, then washed the pieces to find the gold.

Amadou began work. If he could get a good number of rocks out before the other boys came, and there wasn't so much competition, he might be lucky enough to find some gold. Then he could take it to market and sell it. The family badly needed the money it would bring.

Amadou says, "The reason we do this work is that we're trying to survive."

At the surface of the mine, the rocks are crushed and washed to find the gold.

Save the Children is working to help children like Amadou to train to do safer kinds of work, such as carpentry and motorcycle mechanics.

Children caught up in war have the right to be safe

War Today there are more than 50 conflicts going on in the world. Many of these conflicts are civil wars, wars that happen within a country rather than against another country. Most civil wars happen in the poorest countries in the world. They are the result of the struggles between people who want to rule the country. Many children die or are injured in these wars. Nine out of ten people killed in today's wars are civilians who are not directly involved in the fighting.

Forced to fight In recent years, thousands of children under 16 have been child soldiers. This is often because they have lost their families and have nowhere else to go. Their parents may have been killed in the fighting or have somehow become separated from them. Becoming a soldier may be the only way to get food and clothing. Sometimes children start as messengers but end up as soldiers. Children who have been soldiers have seen so much suffering and death that they find it hard to return to normal life.

Aid workers are helping former child soldiers to adjust to ordinary life and to deal with all that they have experienced.

Young boys are often recruited into the armies of poor countries. These recruits are in Afghanistan.

"If it wasn't for the money, I would never have joined the army." Jueir, 11, Democratic

Landmines There may be as many as 110 million landmines lying in wait for people to step on them in over 70 countries. Although they weigh as little as a bag of sweets, they hold enough explosive to blow off a leg if someone steps on one. Around 2,000 people – many of them children – are involved in landmine accidents every month. Around 800 of these will die – the rest are badly hurt. Animals cannot graze and farmers cannot plough land until all the mines have been cleared away.

Refugees When there is war, many people have to leave their homes to find a safer place to live. Women and children are the main people who become refugees or are displaced because of war. Thousands of these refugees are children who have become separated from their families. Being a refugee stops children from doing normal things like going to school and playing with friends.

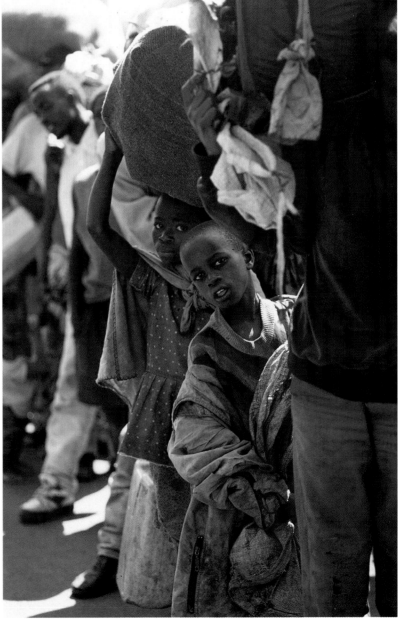

Refugees waiting to return to their home country of Rwanda. Aid workers were on hand to help and protect any children who were travelling alone.

Jueir's story

Jueir lives in Kinshasa, the capital of the Democratic Republic of Congo. Although he is still only 11 years old, he has already been a soldier.

Jueir's father worked for the post office and was sent to a town called Kisangani. Jueir stayed behind with his aunt who continued to look after him when his parents disappeared after war began.

Jueir's aunt is very poor and it was hard for her to look after Jueir properly. He didn't go to school and he had no work. One day he heard that the army paid a monthly salary to all soldiers. Jueir decided to join the army, thinking it would be a good way to earn regular money. He was given a uniform and taught to march. The new recruits were

Jueir, a former child soldier, is much happier now he has left the army.

given jobs to do, like preparing the meals and cutting firewood in the forest. But because they were not given any tools it was hard to do the work. They had to collect water in big containers and carry it long distances to where the soldiers were camping. If they didn't do the work, the boys were beaten.

Then the fighting came to the district where they were camping. Soldiers with serious wounds began to be brought in. Some had lost an arm or a leg – and there were even some dead bodies. The officers said that the boys would be the next to go to fight. Jueir was shocked and afraid. There was so much blood and he didn't want to be killed. So the next time he had to cut wood in the forest, he ran away, back to his aunt.

Now Jueir has joined a local group which is supported by Save the Children. It helps former child soldiers to settle back into ordinary life. The boys are given small plots of land which they use to grow vegetables. They can take vegetables home to help feed their families or they can sell the produce to make money.

These former child soldiers are learning to grow vegetables.

This means that the boys are able to support themselves and their families. The group also helps the children to come to terms with their bad experiences in the army so that they can become part of their family and community again.

Jueir says, "In the army they promised us $100 a month but while I was there I never saw that $100. At least here I see some money and I'm eating."

Growing up safely Although growing up can be difficult, most children and young people receive the love and care they need to become healthy adults. But some children are hurt, neglected or abused by adults or other children. Some younger children may not realise that they are being abused because they have known no other life. Girls often receive more abuse than boys – partly because girls have often been seen as less important than boys. In the past they were often only allowed to work at home or in other people's houses and did not earn much money. This is slowly changing as girls and women challenge the situation.

Bullying Some adults as well as children bully or frighten those who are smaller and weaker than themselves. Often this is because they feel unimportant and see this as a way to show that they are bigger and better than everyone else. Girls are usually not as physically strong as boys and so can be more at risk of being bullied by them.

Children in this Colombian primary school wear masks they have made. They learn how to overcome violence by acting plays about their experience of it.

"If girls become educated and there is equality, then violence will be less."

Bhumisar, 16, Nepal

Discrimination against girls For hundreds of years girls and women have had to suffer particular discrimination by men and boys. They may have been harassed and mistreated. They may have been forbidden to go to school or to work. There are now laws against 'sexual harassment and inequality' in many countries. But still, in many places in the world, men often treat women and girls badly. They do not give them the chance to work and be paid as equals.

Girls in poor countries often suffer from the prejudice of men. As members of a children's parliament, these girls in India are challenging this tradition.

Bhumisar's story

Bhumisar put the broom in the corner. It was still early morning at her home in Nepal, but she had already cleaned the whole house. Her next job was to collect water. The well was half an hour's walk from the village. Bhumisar dreaded the journey. She had to go alone and she was scared all the time she was away from the house. The path went past the small shop where the men gathered to chat and drink tea with each other. When Bhumisar walked past with her water pot, the men would often shout rude things or laugh at her. Sometimes men would follow her and she would have to run to leave them behind.

Bhumisar (on the left) with her friends. She says: "If girls unite in the village, things will continue to change."

There were other places in the village where girls felt scared – the forest, the crossroads, neighbours' houses, even going to one of the festivals could be dangerous. It wasn't only the rude things the men said, sometimes they would attack a girl on her own.

The girls talked to each other about their problems and discovered that many of them felt scared. So they decided to make life safer for themselves. They made a list of the places and times when they felt scared. They talked about their experiences and realised that the men did not respect them or see them as equals. The traditional view was that girls and women were not important, and they should stay at home, cooking and cleaning.

The girls knew that this was wrong, but they also knew it would not be easy to change the way the men thought. So they began by talking with their parents. If their parents understood, then maybe they could talk to other adults and their sons to explain the need for change.

Then the girls began to get the boys at school involved. The boys saw that the girls' exam results were just as good as theirs. They saw the way the girls organised their meetings. They realised that girls were able to do more than cook and clean. They stopped taunting them and saying bad things about them.

The girls now have much more confidence in themselves. They even have the courage to go to the police if the men have been violent.

Members of the girls' group play with some of the younger children in the village.

Bhumisar has taken part in a project called *Safe Spaces for Girls*, which is supported by Save the Children. She says, "I used to be shy and have low self-esteem. We organised a lot of meetings with parents and villagers and my confidence grew."

Children who are surrounded by violence have the right to be safe

Surrounded by violence Children may be surrounded by violence even when there is no war in their country. They may live in an area where the streets are not safe. Maybe there are gangs who 'rule' different streets and fight each other with guns and knives. Innocent people can get hurt because they happen to be in the way of a fight.

Missing school If children on their way to school have to walk past gangs fighting each other, the children may be shot by mistake. Often this danger means that the children are kept at home, so they miss lots of time at school. When this happens, it is hard to catch up with the work they have missed.

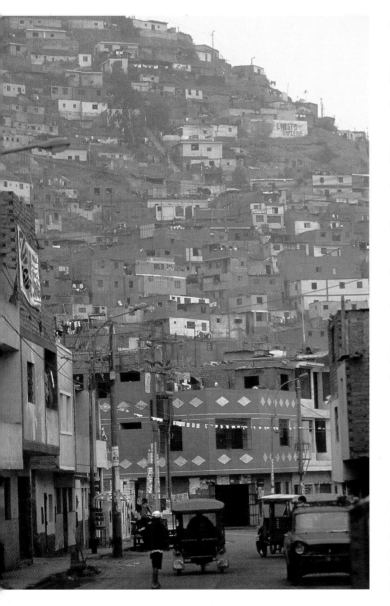

"In this country the guerrilla, the army, the government, the gangs have to learn to live together, but they want to fight each other until there's only one group left."

Wilmer, 11, Colombia

In some places, like this shanty-town in Peru, it can be hard for children playing in the street to stay out of range of the guns of fighting gangs.

Copying the gangs Children who live in districts where gangs threaten people's safety may grow up to copy and then join the gangs. They may not even realise that there is any other way to live.

It can be very hard for someone who lives in a violent area to avoid becoming involved in the violence. For example, fights are often about drugs. A poor person may be tempted to try taking drugs because they think it will help them to cope with being poor. But drugs cost a lot of money. So they sell drugs to other people to try to earn some money. Selling drugs involves them in violence and makes their life worse.

The centre provides street children in Vietnam with a safe place to stay.

Breaking the cycle of violence

Aid organisations support groups that work to help children break away from the violence around them. They show them that a life without violence is better, help them to come off the drugs they have been taking and teach them the skills they will need to get a proper job.

An outreach worker from a project to help street children plays games with them. By making friends with the children, she is able to help them find a safe place to stay.

Rosa's story

Rosa now feels free to go out anywhere she wants. Her old gang realises that she has found a better way to live.

Thirteen-year-old Rosa lives in San Pedro Sula, the second largest city in Honduras, where she lives in one room with her parents and eight brothers and sisters.

Rosa sketched a final twirl on the design. It was perfect. Now she could transfer it on to the T-shirt she had made. She sat back and watched the others around the room. Some were drawing designs; others were sewing. They were her friends.

It was such a relief to have left her old life, as part of a gang, and feel safe instead of scared. 'Why had she been mad enough to join a gang?' she asked herself. Well, it hadn't been easy to stay away. There were ten gangs in the neighbourhood. Her big brother, Roberto, belonged to one, and her sister, Vanessa, had joined another. The family was so poor that there was nothing at home for any of them and at first it had been good to belong to a powerful group. You could get what you wanted and no-one dared stop you because you carried a gun or a knife.

But it was dangerous. The police were often after you – so were other gangs – and you never knew if you would be shot next. It was like being in a trap. The gang leader wanted money

26

every week. There were so many guns and knives. There were drugs. Rosa had been scared nearly all the time.

Then she had met Susana, who worked with a project supported by Save the Children. Susana tried to persuade gang members that they could have a better life. She had told Rosa about the T-shirt-making workshop and Rosa had decided to try it out. It had felt good to be learning proper skills. Rosa was pleased she had stuck to it, even though it had been hard. Now she had an aim for her life. She was going to finish school, buy a sewing machine and set up her own business, making and selling clothes.

Rosa and her sister Vanessa have both managed to leave the gangs that were destroying their lives.

Rosa put her drawing pens away. The best thing about leaving the gang was getting to know her family again. Rosa knew that her mother still loved her although she had suffered so much.

Rosa says, "I feel useful now because I know how to do a few things and feel that people like me. I feel important."

27

Glossary

article A part of a legal document, such as a convention.

child labour The work that children do when it is more than helping with ordinary household jobs.

children's rights The rights that everyone under the age of 18 should have, including the right to life, the right to food, clothes and a place to live, the right to education and health, and the right to be protected from danger.

compensation Money given to make up for something bad that has happened to a person.

conflict A serious disagreement between two or more groups of people which can lead to fighting.

discrimination The unfair treatment of a person because of their race, religion or whether they are a boy or a girl.

displaced people People who have had to leave their homes in an emergency, because of war or a natural disaster, but stay within the same country.

export to sell goods to another country.

exploitation (exploitative) Unfairly taking advantage of a person, for example, if an employer pays children very little for working long hours in a factory.

founded A word meaning started.

harass To worry someone by repeatedly attacking them.

hazardous dangerous.

illegal against the law.

less developed countries Countries which have few industries and in which many people are very poor.

projects Schemes set up to improve life for local people

recruit To persuade someone to join an organisation.

refugees People who leave their home country because they feel unsafe.

representative Someone who is chosen by a group of people to speak on their behalf.

shaft A tunnel in a mine.

street traders People who sell goods on the street rather than in shops.

United Nations An organisation made up of many different countries which was set up in 1945 to promote international peace and cooperation.

Index

Further reading and addresses

Books to read

Save the Children (*Taking Action* series), Heinemann Library/
Save the Children, 2000

Stand Up, Speak Out, Two-Can Publishing, 2001

Packs for teachers

Partners in Rights (a photo pack using creative arts to explore
rights and citizenship for 7-14 year olds), Save the Children,
2000

A Time for Rights (explores citizenship and rights in relation to
the UN Convention on the Rights of the Child, for 9-13 year
olds), Save the Children/UNICEF 2002

Young Citizens (a pack looking at the lives of five young citizens
around the world, for Key Stage 2), Save the Children, 2002

There is a summary version of the UN Convention on the
Rights of the Child at www.childrensrights.ie/yourrights.php

Useful addresses

Save the Children
1 St John's Lane
London EC1
www.savethechildren.org.uk

UNICEF UK
Africa House
64-78 Kingsway
London WC2B 6NB
www.unicef.org

Save the Children Australia
Level 3
20 Council St
Hawthorn East
Vic 3123
www.savethechildren.org.au

UNICEF Australia
Level 3
303 Pitt St
Sydney
NSW 2000
www.unicef.com.au